More Fairy Poems

Clare Bevan lives in a cobwebby house with her husband, Martin, her son, Ben, a family of stick insects and a brown hamster called Malteser. She used to be a teacher, but now she spends most of her time writing poems. Her favourite hobbies are acting, wearing hats and riding around her village on a big purple tricycle.

Lara Jones lives in a tiny cottage by a misty hill with her husband, Shaun, and baby daughter. She likes painting pictures, eating Marmite on toast and day-dreaming.

Other books from Macmillan

FAIRY POEMS
By Clare Bevan
Illustrated by Lara Jones

PRINCESS POEMS
By Clare Bevan
Illustrated by Lara Jones

MERMAID POEMS
By Clare Bevan
Illustrated by Lara Jones

SPACE POEMS
Chosen by Gaby Morgan
Illustrated by Jane Eccles

More Fairy Poems

By Clare Bevan

Illustrated by Lara Jones

MACMILLAN CHILDREN'S BOOKS

*For all my readers – may your favourite dreams come true.
And for Mich and Betty, the good fairies of
Frensham Road. C.B.*

To India Rose with fairy dust. L.J.

First published 2006 by Macmillan Children's Books
an imprint of Macmillan Publishers Limited
20 New Wharf Road, London N1 9RR
Basingstoke and Oxford
www.panmacmillan.com

Associated companies throughout the world

ISBN-13: 978-0330-43935-0
ISBN-10: 0-330-43935-9

Text copyright © Clare Bevan 2006
Illustrations copyright © Lara Jones 2006

The right of Clare Bevan and Lara Jones to be identified as the
author and illustrator of this book has been asserted by them in accordance
with the Copyright, Designs and Patents Act 1988.

1 3 5 7 9 8 6 4 2

A CIP catalogue record for this book is available from the British Library.

Printed and bound in Great Britain by Mackays of Chatham plc, Kent.

Contents

Fairy Gold

*Clare found this poem hiding inside her
piggy bank*

Fairy gold, fairy gold
Fleetingly lingers,
Tickles your skin
As it slips through your fingers.
Sparky as starlight
It glints in your hand,
Melts in a moment
And scatters like sand.
Teasy as raindrops
It trickles away,
Misty as moonbeams
It fades into grey.
Rarer than unicorns,
Lighter than laughter,
Fairy gold shines
In your mind
Ever after.

What the Springtime Fairy Wears

This poem fell out of Clare's best boots on a rainy day

A blossom-pink petticoat,
Rainbow-striped dress,
A cloudy-white shawl
That is made (can you guess?)
With fluff she untangled
From little lamb-tails,
Puddle-grey wellies
With silvery scales,
A hat that is pinned
With a duck's yellow feather
And a leafy umbrella
For showery weather.

What the Summer Fairy Wears

Clare found this poem pinned to her favourite flowery top

Her skirt is the colour
Of holiday sand,
Her blue seashell buttons
Are painted by hand,
Her sunshade is patterned
With butterfly wings,
Her nettle-green sandals
Are made without stings
And her wide, shady hat
Has been woven from hay
For the fairy who dances
On sunbeams all day.

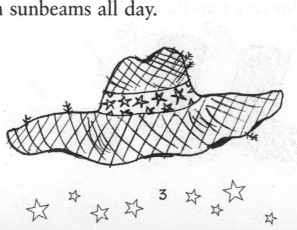

What the Autumn Fairy Wears

Clare rescued this poem from the middle of a
blackberry bush

A cobweb coat as pale as fog,
Twiggy buttons (from a log),
Tights dyed blue with juicy berries,
Gloves as red as glossy cherries,
An oak-leaf hat in golden shades
(Spellbound so it never fades)
And spiky shoes with ivy laces,
Light and tight for treetop races.

The Lily-Pad Prance

This poem was given to Clare by a rather timid frog

Oh, the Fairies of the River
Like a shiver, quiver dance,
But the Fairies of the Pond prefer
The Lily-Pad Prance . . .
They bustle past the beetles,
They rustle past the frogs,
They tangle and they dangle
Over water-weedy logs.

Oh, the Fairies of the Mountain
Like a snowy, blowy dance,
But the Fairies of the Pond prefer
The Lily-Pad Prance . . .
They flurry with the goldfish,
They scurry with the voles,
They squiggle and they wriggle
Through the water-ratty holes.

Oh, the Fairies of the Garden
Like a pretty, flitty dance,
But the Fairies of the Pond prefer
The Lily-Pad Prance . . .
They dash across the ripples,
They splash across the stones,
They giggle and they jiggle
On their water-lily thrones.

Oh, the Fairies of the Moonlight
Like a lazy, hazy dance,
But the Fairies of the Pond prefer
THE LILY-PAD PRANCE.

The Naughty Fairies' Song

Clare found this poem when she was looking for a lost sock

Some fairies are charming and gentle and
　　sweet,
Some fairies go dancing on little light feet.

But we are the fairies
Who tangle your hair,
Who jumble your jigsaws
When no one is there,
Who hide your best treasures,
Who muddle your socks,
Who tumble your toys
From their big, tidy box,
Who tickle your hamster,
Who startle your cat,
Who drop spiky stones
On your soft bedside mat,
Who scamper and giggle
Like rascally mice,
Who aren't very dainty,
Who aren't very nice.

Some fairies just twinkle and skip in the
  sun,
But WE are the fairies who have the most
  FUN.

Two, Four,
Six, Eight . . .

Clare found this poem inside a box of counters

Two Christmas Fairies –
    Hang frost on the trees,
Four Summer Fairies –
    Buy nectar from bees,
Six Bedtime Fairies –
    Tell magical tales,
Eight Seaside Fairies –
    Sing songs with the whales,
Ten Frisky Fairies –
    Fly swifter than swallows,
Twelve Birthday Fairies –
    Weave happy tomorrows.
Lots of Good Fairies –
    Make wishes come true,
Hundreds of Fairies –
    Are hiding near YOU,
Thousands of Fairies –
    Will smile when you call . . .

And . . .

One Quiet Fairy Is Queen of Us All.

Tooth-Palace Dreams

This poem popped into Clare's mind when she woke from a dream

Tooth Palace tall
In my Tooth-Palace dream,
Why do your turrets
So sleepily gleam?

"My walls and my towers all glittery
       white
Were built by the fairies who follow the
       light
Of the pale winter moon and the
       shivering stars
To dark city windows protected by bars.
To deep, gloomy caverns. To lighthouses
       round.
To igloos. To tree houses far above
       ground.
To boats on the river. To homes in the
       hills.
To tents in the forest where rain softly
       spills.

To beautiful castles. To huts with no
    bread . . .
WHEREVER a note has been placed by
    the bed,
WHEREVER a tooth has been placed on
    a chair,
Or twisted in tissue, or hidden with care.
As silent as moth-wings, the tooth fairies
    find
Your present and leave a small payment
    behind,
Then vanish like snowflakes and scurry
    away
To make my walls higher and finer each
    day.
THAT'S why my turrets
So sleepily gleam,"
The Tooth Palace said
In my Tooth-Palace dream.

What Do Fairies Ride?

Clare would really like to ride on a heron

The quietest fairies ride barn owls
As soft as a flurry of snow,
The fiercest fairies ride falcons,
Or sometimes a cackling crow.

The cleverest fairies ride magpies,
The tiniest fairies ride wrens,
The happiest fairies ride songbirds,
The noisiest fairies ride hens.

The sleepiest fairies ride dormice,
The funniest fairies ride frogs,
The bravest of fairies ride whirlwinds,
Or cling to the collars of dogs.

The fairies who grant all our wishes,
They ride on the greyest of doves,
The fairies who ride on the phoenix
Wear feathery fireproof gloves.

The Fairies of Morning ride skylarks.
The Fairies of Darkness ride bats,
The Fairies of Water ride fishes,
The Fairies of Moonlight ride cats.

But the daintiest rider who soars through
the sky
Is the Fairy of May on her blue
butterfly.

Three Wishes

If Clare could have three wishes, she would ask for three wishing wells

Three wishes!
Three wishes!
What will YOU choose?
Honey or
Money or
Flyaway shoes?

Princes or
Quinces or
Rivers of gold?
Parcels or
Castles or
Starlight to hold?

Dresses or
Tresses of
Ebony hair?
Flowers or
Showers of
Jewels to share?

Songbirds or
Long words or
Secrets to keep?
Faces or
Places to
See in your sleep?

Potions or
Notions to
Make you feel clever?
New gloves or
True-loves for
Ever and ever?

Treasures or
Pleasures too
Precious to lose?
Three wishes!
Three wishes!
What will you choose?

Home Sweet Home

Clare once saw this spotty toadstool in a quiet wood

The fairy lives in a toadstool tall,
With a spotty roof and a scarlet wall
And two wide windows made of ice
And a doorway chewed by helpful mice
And a steep white stairway, long and thin,
And a grassy mat that says
COME IN!

A Scrumptious Puzzle

Can you find the Fluttery Fairy's favourite food?

Fluttery Fairy! What do you eat?
Anything pretty and anything sweet . . .
Icing's enticing on
Rose-petal Pies,
Young yellow pollen with
Cowslip Surprise,
Apple-juice Jelly or Daisy Delight,
Kept under hedges and
Eaten at night.

What is the very best food of them all?
Blossom-pink FAIRY CAKE, dainty and
small.

This Little Fairy . . .

Fairy mothers sing this song when they count their babies' toes

This little fairy paints the rainbows,
This little fairy shakes the snow,
This little fairy makes the shadows,
This little fairy likes to glow,
But THIS little fairy caught a Big Bad
        Breeze
By the end of his tiniest toe!

(Fairy babies giggle
When their little toes are wiggled.)

The Fairy Godmother's Daughter

This poem was written on a rose petal and dropped into Clare's teacup

My mother grants wishes
For sleepy princesses –
Wonderful weddings and
Glittery dresses.

My mother grants wishes
For girls who are lonely –
Huge pumpkin coaches for
One evening only.

My mother grants wishes
For girls trapped in towers –
Hair long as waterfalls,
Magical powers.

Oh, when will my mother
Grant wishes for me?
(I just want a wand
And a tame bumblebee.)

Fairy Letters

These letters were once sent to Clare and her lazy old cat

Dear Giants
(In your Giant House),
Have you seen
My racing mouse?
His eyes are sharp,
His fur is black.
If you find him –
Send him back.

Dear Giants
(And your Giant Cat),
My mouse came home!
He's grown quite fat
And rather slow
But never mind –
Thank you all
For being kind.

Dear Giants,
Here is your REWARD!
A magic cake
(It's slightly gnawed).
Now – take one bite
And make three wishes.
PS My mouse
Sends love and kisses.

The Fairyland Zoo

Clare has searched her garden, but she hasn't found the zoo yet

When fairies fly off to the Fairyland Zoo
They ride on a dragonfly. That's what they
    do . . .

They don't like the wasps,
Who are stripy and scary.
They squeal at the shrew,
Who is horribly hairy.
They peep at the mole,
Who has mud on his paws.
They feed the big beetles,
Who clatter their jaws.
They clap when the grasshopper
Makes a HUGE jump.
They sit on the centipede
(Bumpety-bump!).
They queue up to eat
At the Bumble Cafe –
Warm honey buns
On an ivy-leaf tray.

They buy spider yo-yos
And toys that can hop
(Flies, fleas and frogs)
From the Garden-World Shop.

Then the fairies ride home from the
       Fairyland Zoo
On a friendly old dragonfly. That's what
       they do.

The Toyshop Fairies

Clare found this poem inside a Noah's Ark that belonged to her Granny

The Toyshop Fairies like to float
All aboard a wooden boat . . .

Its dusty deck
Is rather full
Of painted pigs,
A cow, a bull,
A pair of bears,
Two ducks, two dogs,
Two elephants,
Two spotty frogs,
Two tigers twitching
Stripy tails,
Two tall giraffes,
Two tiny snails,
Two pythons (thin),
Two hippos (fat)
And one old sailor
With his cat.
And though they're

SQUASHED
And squeezed all day,
The Toyshop Fairies
Smile and say . . .

"We're happy in our ship-shape stable –
At least we've learned our two-times-
     table."

The Rainforest Fairy

Rainforests are full of leafy hiding places for fairies

She has . . .

A dress as bright
As lizard scales,
Hair that curls
Like monkey tails,
Shadow stripes
Across her skin,
Teeth as pointy
As a pin
And golden eyes
That blink and gaze
Lazily through
Heat and haze.

She . . .

Swings from vines
As strong as wires,
Listens to the
Tree-frog choirs,
Laughs at snakes
And snappy things,
Rescues moon-moths,
Mends their wings,
Then spirals round
The nest she weaves
From parrot feathers,
Patterned leaves.

She . . .

Lives below a great green dome
And sings, "I love my forest home."

The Fairy of the Bees

A big furry bee buzzed into Clare's room and told her this fairy story

She charms the bees that roam her land
(Stripy coats and spiteful stings).
She feeds them nectar from her hand
(Warning buzz and warrior wings).

She tells them where the bluebell grows
(Furry coats and faithful stings).
She leads them to the wild white rose
(Friendly buzz and folded wings).

They place their presents at her feet
(Wands as sharp as insect stings,
Bowls of honey, dark and sweet,
And velvet shoes with waxy wings).

The Fire Fairy

If you are lucky, perhaps you might
Spot this fairy on Bonfire Night

The Fire Fairy loves November.

She twirls around in her flame-coloured
    dress
Until her black dancing boots spark like
    coals
And her pale hair streams about her
As wispily as smoke.

Then she flickers through the foggy night
To watch the Catherine wheels whirl like
    galaxies,
Or to ride on rockets that splatter the sky
With starry flowers.

"Crackle and curl,"
She sings to the bonfires
As she swoops from garden
To garden.
"Scatter and swirl."

And with one swish of her thin grey
    wand
She decorates the dark
With scarlet fireflies
And spells of wonder.

Do You Believe?

Clare always claps her hands when she goes to see
Peter Pan. Do you?

Do you believe in fairies?
Do you believe they are near?
Just on the edges of Maybe,
The borders of Nowhere and Here.

Do you believe in toadstools
With windows that quietly close?
Do you believe in dancers
Who spin on the spike of a rose?

Do you believe in wishes
And gifts that are given in threes?
Do you believe in castles
That gleam in the hollows of trees?

If you believe in fairies
And if you believe in their song,
Then magic will sparkle inside you
Like treasure, your whole life long.

The Rainy-Day Fairy

Clare thinks she once saw this fairy splashing through a puddle

"Oh," cried the fairy
Who brings us the rain,
"Everyone hates me,
From Scotland to Spain!
They grumble and grizzle,
They cough and complain.

They greet my best puddles
With scowls and with sighs,
They frown at my beautiful
Blustery skies . . .
And even the children
Have tears in their eyes."

"Cheer up," said a fairy
All dressed like a queen,
In red, blue and yellow
And purple and green,
"Without you, my RAINBOW
Would never be seen."

Blue and Green

Clare found this poem at Birdworld. It was pinned to a peacock's feather

"Blue and green should never be seen
Without a colour in between . . ."

But no one told the hills and sky,
And no one told the dragonfly.

No one warned (and no one should)
The bluebells in the Fairy Wood.

No one murmured mournful words
To fairy riders. Or their birds.

No one told the fairies who
Dance in gowns of green and blue.

And no one dared to tell their Queen.
(Her brand-new boots are blue and green!)

PS If Fairy Queens wear green and blue,
Then I think YOU can wear them too.

The Littlest Fairy

Clare found this poem curled inside a dented thimble

The littlest fairy that anyone knew
Was Flittery-Flutter-Forget-Me-Not Blue.

Her house was a thimble of copper and
    tin
With cobwebby curtains, incredibly thin.

Her bed was one half of a hazelnut shell,
Her wand was a splinter (or so I've heard
    tell).

Her voice was as soft as a butterfly's call,
Her courage was mighty (although she was
    small).

She hunted with owls and with leathery
    bats,
She feared neither foxes nor scraggy old
    cats.

She battled with beetles and big
    squeaky mice.
They tried to surprise her. They didn't try
    twice!

And she lived in a garden that's somewhere
    near YOU,
Did Flittery-Flutter-Forget-Me-Not Blue.

The Fairy Fairground

Clare found this poem fixed to a nutshell, just like a paper sail

In our fairground
You can ride:
The Ivy Swings,
The Treetop Slide,
The Nutshell Ship
(That sails across
The Swampy Pond),
The Bouncy Moss
(Remember to
Remove your shoes),
The Hosepipe Flume
(Expect long queues),
The Mono-Snail
(It's smooth and slow),
The Haunted Hive
(Where glow-worms glow),
The Bumper Beetles
(Fast and funny),
The Big-Bee Racers
(Win that honey!),

The Bungee Spiders
(Watch them drop)
And BEST of all –
THE LEAP-FROG HOP!

Glow-Worm Poem

*Clare found this poem in the dusty cupboard
where she keeps her torch*

My glow-worm glows
The whole night through –
It's what a glow-worm
Likes to do.
He lights my path
Between the trees
And NEVER needs
New batteries.

The Easter Fairy

This poem fell out of a hollow Easter Egg!

This fairy is the best of friends
With Easter Rabbit, so she sends
Surprising presents – yellow gloves
And hot-cross buns (a thing he LOVES).

Together, they make special sweets –
Sugar flowers, spring-time treats
For Easter Day. And then they hide
Eggs for you. Indoors. Outside.

But when they've finished, I'm afraid,
They like to taste the eggs they've made
And sometimes (you should warn your
    mums)
They leave a trail of chocolate crumbs.

Fairy Photographs

Clare has tried and TRIED to photograph the fairies. No luck so far . . .

When you try to sneak and spy,
Snipper-snap,
We will smile and flutter by,
Flitter-flap.

We will swish our spiky wands,
Sparkle-flash,
We will skim across your ponds,
Dazzle-dash.

We will light the leafy trees,
Gleam-and-glow,
We will freeze the morning breeze,
Sleet-and-snow.

We will ride our speedy mice,
Spin-back-soon,
We will dance in circles TWICE
Round-the-moon.

When you print your photographs
What is there?
Falling leaves and stony paths
And empty air.

Bring on the Band

Clare has often heard the birds and insects
practising their special royal fanfare in her garden

Daffodils, trumpet!
And ring, bluebells, ring!
Bring on the band
For the Queen and the King!

Fairies, find petals!
Find leaves red and green!
Flutter your flags
For the King and the Queen!

Nightingales, whistle!
You grasshoppers, sing!
Practise your tunes
For the Queen and the King!

Cheer when you see them!
And wave as they go –
Tan-tara! Flutter!
Tra-la-la! BRAVO!

Snow-Fairy Song

Snow Fairies are very rare these days – but maybe you'll see one if you make a winter wish

Snow Fairy, Snow Fairy,
Where do you go
When the North Wind sleeps
And the warm winds blow?

"Over the rivers,
Over the trees,
Over the hills
On a whirly breeze,
Over the mountains,
Over the seas,
Over the clouds
Where the blizzards tease,
Over the lands
Where the snowmen sneeze,
To my nice ice home
Where I freeze, freeze, FREEZE!"

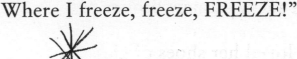

What Cinderella's Fairy Godmother Said . . .

Clare wouldn't ask for glass slippers. She likes fluffy ones better

"The spells I enjoyed the BEST of all
Were the ones I cast for the Prince's Ball.

I turned a pumpkin into gold,
With comfy seats and wheels that rolled.

I gave the kitchen mice a fright –
I changed them into horses (white).

I caught a lizard, green and fat,
And dressed him in a coachman's hat.

I gave the girl a sky-blue gown
Instead of raggy scraggy brown.

But oh! I loved her shoes of glass
That danced away across the grass.

That's why they didn't fade away.
(And why she wears them still. Today!)"

Eyelash Spell

*Clare whispers this little spell whenever she blows
an eyelash away*

Eyelash, eyelash
On my cheek,
Softly rise and
Swiftly seek
A fairy who is
Good and kind,
Who knows my heart,
Who reads my mind,
And let her grant
My wish today –
Eyelash, eyelash,
    FLY AWAY.

*(But no one knows why the fairies like to collect
eyelashes.)*

A Fairy Alphabet

Young fairies learn this poem before they write their first letters

Aiming high and swooping low,
Building castles in the snow,
Casting spells with shiny thorns,
Drifting over garden lawns,
Eating berries dipped in honey,
Finding teeth and leaving money,
Gliding on a summer breeze,
Hiding inside hollow trees,
Icing tiny fairy cakes,
Jumping over moonlit lakes,
Keeping still when danger's near,
Leaping with the fallow deer,
Making children's dreams come true,
Nursing injured mouse and shrew,
Opening a toadstool door,
Pirouetting round the floor,

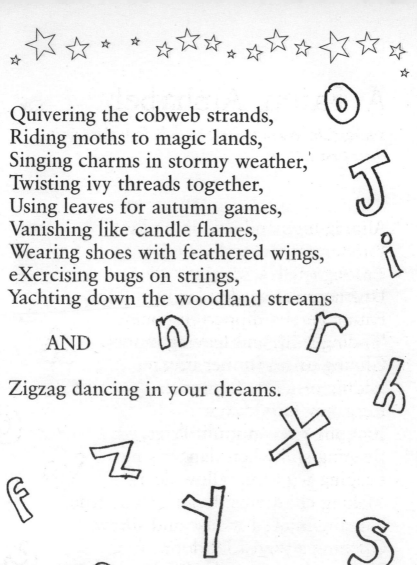

Quivering the cobweb strands,
Riding moths to magic lands,
Singing charms in stormy weather,
Twisting ivy threads together,
Using leaves for autumn games,
Vanishing like candle flames,
Wearing shoes with feathered wings,
eXercising bugs on strings,
Yachting down the woodland streams

AND

Zigzag dancing in your dreams.

Fairy Limericks

The fairies say these poems just for fun

The Fairy of Wintry Wood
Sewed snowflakes as well as she could
(Not white, as you'd think –
But strawberry pink!
And they tasted amazingly good).

The Fairy of Sand-by-the-Sea
Ate ice cream for breakfast and tea.
She had cornets to crunch
For supper and lunch
And she giggled, "Who's greedy? Not me!"

Wishes and Fairies

*Clare once wished for a book of poems – but she
was given a glittery pen*

The city girl wished for beauty,
But her fairy godmother gave her
A spotty old mirror instead.
Every morning the girl gazed at her
    speckled face
And every evening she grumbled,
"My fairy must be too busy or too dizzy
To help me at all."

After one year and one day,
Her mirror shone clearer than mountain
    water
And the city girl saw her own sweet self.
"How beautiful I am!" she cried.
"And who needs a fairy godmother
    anyway?"

The country girl wished for riches,
But her fairy godmother gave her
A pair of foggy glasses instead.
Every morning the girl gazed at a grey
    world
And every evening she grumbled,
"My fairy must be too gloomy or too
    doomy
To help me at all."

After one year and one day,
Her glasses vanished like morning mist
And the country girl saw her own
    dazzling garden.
"How rich I am!" she cried.
"And who needs a fairy godmother
    anyway?"

The dreamy girl wished for a handsome
        prince,
But her fairy godmother gave her
A statue of glittering glass instead.
Every morning the girl gazed at her silent
        hero
And every evening she sighed,
"My fairy must be too muddled or too
        fuddled
To help me at all."

After one year and one day,
A young man knocked on her door.
He was not a prince,
He was not exactly handsome,
But he WAS her best friend in all the
        world.
"How lucky I am!" she cried
"And who needs a fairy godmother
        anyway?"

MORAL: When wishes are granted,
Expect a surprise
        Fairies are sneaky
        But awfully WISE.

The Fairy Library

Clare found this poem inside a little book with rose-petal pages

Books to lend and
Books to borrow . . .

Some bring laughter. Some bring sorrow.
Some are old as story kings.
Some are made from insect wings.
Some are filled with sing-song spells.
Some have grassy garden smells.
Some have writing wild and swirly.
Some have pages lost, or curly.
Some will grumble when you shake
      them.
Some will sparkle when you wake them.
Some show scary, human faces,
Talking creatures, misty places.
Some can roar and squeak and bark.
Some will shiver in the dark.
Some will burn at break of day,
Some will flap and fly away
Faster than a swift or swallow.

Some will show the path to follow
Round the world and back tomorrow . . .

Books to lend and
Books to borrow.

A Magical Puzzle

I hope you can solve this one faster than Clare did. She took AGES

My first is in DAISY but not in CHAIN,

My second's in RAINDROP but not in RAIN,

My third is in NETTLE but not in STING,

My fourth is in APRIL but not in SPRING,

My fifth is in FLOWER but not in ROSE,

My WHOLE is a MAGIC that glints and glows.

ANSWER: If you search this puzzle well,
             You will spot my hidden SPELL.

The Hollow Tree

Hollow trees are the BEST places to look for fairy tracks

The branches of the hollow tree
Have doors we hardly ever see
And hidden holes the fairies share
With squirrels (who are welcome there
Because their tails are soft and warm
In blizzard and in thunderstorm).

Old magpie nests are used to store
The treasures of the forest floor –
Pearly buttons, precious rings
Lost by long-forgotten kings
And phoenix feathers (red and rare)
To line the cloaks the fairies wear.

Below the leaves, the children ride
A helter-skelter tree-trunk slide,
While older fairies doze on beds
That swing from silky spider threads,
And higher still, on hoverflies,
The guards watch out for human spies.

A Spell to Mend Broken Wings

This spell will work on all sorts of flying creatures – from bats and bees to fishes and fairies

Sycamore, sycamore, sycamore seed,
Spin me the magic of river and reed,
Spin me the spells of the dandelion
    flower,
Spin me a secret in less than an hour.

Bring me the bubbles of fish in a brook,
Bring me the feather that wrote an old
    book,
Bring me the perfume of blossoms that
    blow,
Bring me the shivery whispers of snow.

Comfort the moth as it falls from the sky,
Comfort the beetle, the tumbling fly,
Comfort the bat in the deepest of caves,
Comfort the seabird who battles the waves.

Rescue the hawk who is hunted at dawn,
Rescue the crow on the cat-haunted
    lawn
Rescue the phoenix, the great flying
    horse,
Rescue the trembling fairy (of course).

Send them and mend them by sunlight
    and rain,
Send them all fluttering freely again,
Send them like stars over water and weed,
Sycamore, sycamore, sycamore seed.

When Wands
Go Wrong

Clare thinks that the fairies have fun when their wands go wrong

When wands go wrong,
When spells are lost,
What is the magical, tragical cost?

WELL . . .

Pumpkins grow smaller
Than hummingbird eggs.
Mice become horseflies
With galloping legs.
Spinning wheels whirl
Across time, across space,
To wrap the whole palace
In curtains of lace.
Ragged old dresses
Are flappy brown bats.
Lamps (when you rub them)
Start purring like cats.

Straw isn't spun
Into gold for a king,
But bright yellow parrots
Who chatter and sing.
As for the Frog Prince –
He still wears a crown,
But his bride is a rat
In a waterweed gown.

OH!

Salt becomes sugar and short becomes long
When spells are lost,
When wands go wrong.

The Song of the Warrior Fairy

Warning – please don't EVER try to catch the Warrior Fairy!

I'm not your lily fairy
In a pale petal skirt.
I'm not your frilly fairy –
I wear trousers and a shirt.
I'm not your silly fairy
Who is scared of dark and dirt –
For I'm the Warrior Fairy
And my spiky sword can HURT.

I'm not your pretty fairy
Who is kind and shy and nice.
I'm not your flitty fairy –
I have captured gangs of mice.
I'm not your witty fairy,
But my words are sharp as ice –
For I'm the Warrior Fairy
And I'll tame you in a trice.

I'm not your neatest fairy,
I am fed from broken dishes.
I'm not your fleetest fairy –
Though my spears are fast as fishes.
I'm not your sweetest fairy
When my wand of bramble swishes –
But if you bring me silver pins
I'll grant your dearest wishes.

Grey-Cloud

Clare once knew a quiet teacher who was just like Fairy Grey-Cloud

The quietest teacher in the whole school
Was Fairy Grey-Cloud
Her wings were so faded and delicate
She would fly only on the warmest of days,
And she rode to school on a bumblebee
    called Hum,
Who took grains of sugar from her
    pockets.

Her beetle-shell shoes made no sound
As she tiptoed around the classrooms,
And when she sang her voice was so
    whispery-thin
The fairy-children leaned forward
On their pointy elbows
To listen, listen . . .
But even then her words seem to come
From a far and forgotten land.

She seldom grew angry
Or made her willow-wand crackle,
Yet everyone fell silent when she drifted
    by,
And the sun seemed to shine more brightly
If she smiled.

"What is your secret?"
Asked Fairy Tangle-String,
Who taught frost-craft and spider-sports
To wriggly, giggly classes.
But Fairy Grey-Cloud only winked.

There was no need to say a word.

She was just
MAGICAL.

Ten Fairy Jokes

These jokes were all made up by Fairy Tangle-String's Class

1. Which fairy likes to climb trees?
   IVY
2. Which fairy likes to float on the pond?
   LILY
3. Which fairy wears a nutshell on her head?   HAZEL
4. Which fairy wears a Christmas leaf on her head?   HOLLY
5. Which fairy wears a purple petal on her head?   VIOLET
6. Which fairy wears a pink petal on her head?   ROSIE
7. Which fairy picks all the flowers?
   POSY
8. What does the fairy call her sleepy slug?   DOZY
9. What does the fairy call her cuddly bug?   COSY

AND . . .

10. What do you call a fairy who keeps asking questions? NOSY!

Ten Fairy Facts

These facts were given to Clare by a bumblebee called Hum

1. The best spider to use for tree-falling is the Wolf Spider. (She's much friendlier than she sounds.)
2. Fairies like to wear conker-shell helmets for games lessons. (The straps are made from sticky cobwebs.)
3. The Pond Fairy has two new babies. The girl is called Lake-Lily and the boy is called Frog-Rider.
4. The biggest tooth the fairies have collected this year came from a young polar bear called Growler.
5. Flittery-Flutter-Forget-Me-Not-Blue says the secret of long life is one new fairy joke every day.
6. The Fairy Queen's favourite book is *One Hundred Amazing Eyelash Spells.*

7. The Snow Fairy hurt her wings in a Christmas blizzard, but she was given a really good spell and now she can fly faster than ever.

8. Fairies NEVER wear leafy hats when they dance with a hamster.

9. The Fairy of the Bees says that stripy velvet slippers will be very popular this winter.

10. If you hear jingly music at the end of your garden this summer, please don't worry. It's only the Fairy Fairground.

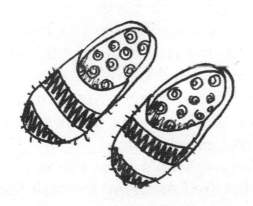

CLARE BEVAN

Princess Poems

Could you be a princess?

A gorgeous collection of poems filled with tips on how to behave like a princess, meet the right prince and avoid the dangers posed by wicked stepmothers, dragons and unhappy fairy godmothers.

If You Were a Princess

If YOU were a princess, what would YOU ride?
A small, metal dragon
with cogwheels inside?
A horse with white feathers
and hooves of black glass?
A silvery unicorn
pounding the grass?
A fluttering carpet
that chases the bats?
A big, golden pumpkin
With coachmen like rats?
A castle that sways
on an elephant's back?
A long, steamy train
Going clickety clack?
Or a ship with blue sails
And YOUR name on the side?
If YOU were a princess, what would YOU ride?

A selected list of titles available from Macmillan Children's Books

The prices shown below are correct at the time of going to press. However, Macmillan Publishers reserves the right to show new retail prices on covers which may differ from those previously advertised.

Clare Bevan

Fairy Poems	0 330 43352 0	£3.99
Princess Poems	0 330 43389 X	£3.99
Mermaid Poems	0 330 43785 2	£3.99

All Pan Macmillan titles can be ordered from our website, www.panmacmillan.com, or from your local bookshop and are also available by post from:

Bookpost, PO Box 29, Douglas, Isle of Man IM99 1BQ
Credit cards accepted. For details:
Telephone: +44(0)1624 677237
Fax: +44(0)1624 670923
Email: bookshop@enterprise.net
www.bookpost.co.uk

Free postage and packing in the United Kingdom